DINOSAUR DATA

BY NANCY HONOVICH

PUBLISHED BY TANGERINE PRESS, AN IMPRINT OF SCHOLASTIC INC.,
557 BROADWAY, NEW YORK, NY 10012
SCHOLASTIC CANADA LTD., MARKHAM, ONTARIO
SCHOLASTIC AUSTRALIA PTY. LTD, GOSFORD NSW
SCHOLASTIC NEW ZEALAND LTD., GREENMOUNT, AUCKLAND
GROLIER INTERNATIONAL, INC., MAKATI CITY, PHILIPPINES

PRODUCED BY BECKER&MAYER!
11120 NE 33RD PLACE, SUITE 101
BELLEVUE, WA 98004
WWW.BECKERMAYER.COM

IF YOU HAVE QUESTIONS OR COMMENTS ABOUT THIS BOOK, PLEASE VISIT WWW.BECKERMAYER.COM/CUSTOMERSERVICE AND CLICK ON CUSTOMER SERVICE REQUEST FORM.

EDITED BY BEN GROSSBLATT
DESIGNED BY TYLER FREIDENRICH
DESIGN ASSISTANCE BY CORTNY HELMICK, RYAN HOBSON, AND SHAHMIN MAHMOOD
ILLUSTRATIONS BY CONCEPTOPOLIS: FRONT COVER, TITLE PAGE, MAIN ILLUSTRATIONS; RYAN HOBSON: SILHOUETTES, BACK COVER; MARC DANDO: 4, 6, 7, 8 (CLAW AND SNOUT), 10, 12, 13, 14, 21, 23, 24, 25, 26, 27, 29, 30 (SKULL), 32, 33, 38, 44 (CRESTS AND WING BONES), 46, 54, 56, 58, 59, 60; NATHAN HALE: 34, 35, 52; PETER BULL STUDIOS: 18; MICHAEL KOMARCK: 28; DAVIDE BONADONNA: 62.
PRODUCTION MANAGEMENT BY LARRY WEINER
IMAGE RESEARCH BY ZENA CHEW
FACTS CHECKED BY PAUL BECK
SPECIAL THANKS TO ROSANNA BROCKLEY, SHANE HARTLEY AND CATHERINE CHIEN

IMAGE CREDITS:
GETTY IMAGES: PAGE 14, FOSSIL COELOPHYSIS © KEN LUCAS/VISUALS UNLIMITED; PAGE 16, FOSSIL COMPSOGNATHUS © KEN LUCAS/VISUALS UNLIMITED; PAGE 41, PACHYCEPHALOSAURUS FIGHT © DE AGOSTINI PICTURE LIBRARY. WIKIMEDIA COMMONS: PAGE 36, MUTTABURRASAURUS, MATT MARTYNIUK; PAGE 38, OVIRAPTOR EGGS, GERBIL; PAGE 40, PACHYCEPHALOSAURUS SKULL, FUNKMUNK; PAGE 56, THERIZINOSAURUS CLAW, WOUDLOPER.

TP4025-1 7/10
PRINTED IN USA

10 9 8 7 6 5 4 3 2 1

ISBN: 978-0-545-24971-3

40

08133

COMPLIES WITH CPSIA

TABLE OF CONTENTS

[ARCHAEOPTERYX]

(AR-kee-OP-ter-iks) "Ancient wing"

Archaeopteryx, which boasted feathered wings, is sometimes referred to as the first bird.

VITAL STATS

LENGTH: ABOUT 1.5 FT. (.5 M)
WEIGHT: 1.1 LB. (.5 KG)
PERIOD: MIDDLE TO LATE JURASSIC
PLACE: GERMANY

QUICK FACTS

▸ Unlike birds today, Archaeopteryx had jaws with small, cone-shaped teeth that could cut larger prey into smaller pieces.

▸ Archaeopteryx had three bony claws on each wing.

Bony claws

DINO-SIZE

Archaeopteryx—a birdlike creature—was about the size of a crow.

CROW

STRENGTH: ▮▮▮▮▮▯▯▯▯▯
SPEED: ▮▮▮▯▯▯▯▯▯▯
INTELLIGENCE: ▮▮▮▮▮▯▯▯▯▯

SPECIAL FEATURE: Flight

▶ Because its shoulder joints were angled sideways, Archaeopteryx was able to lift its wings high above its back while flying.

▶ Feathers on its hind legs may have provided the creature with lift.

▶ Its long feathered tail kept Archaeopteryx stable during flight.

1 FT. (.3 M)

ARCHAEOPTERYX

BAROSAURUS

(BEAR-uh-SOR-us) "Heavy lizard"

The enormous Barosaurus could have used its great size to tackle much smaller attackers.

Vital Stats

LENGTH: ABOUT 88 FT. (27 M)
WEIGHT: 60,000 LBS.
(27,200 KG)
PERIOD: LATE JURASSIC
PLACE: WESTERN NORTH
AMERICA, EAST AFRICA

Quick Facts

▸ Barosaurus is believed to have had a small skull with short peglike teeth, which it used to eat plants.

▸ Barosaurus might have swallowed stones called gastroliths, which would grind the food as it traveled down the dinosaur's digestive tract.

Gastroliths

Dino-Size

Barosaurus was nearly the length of the largest living animal—the blue whale.

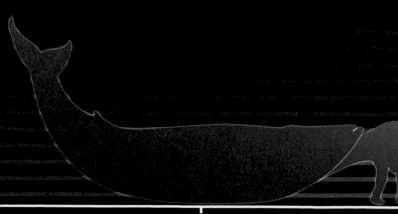

BLUE WHALE

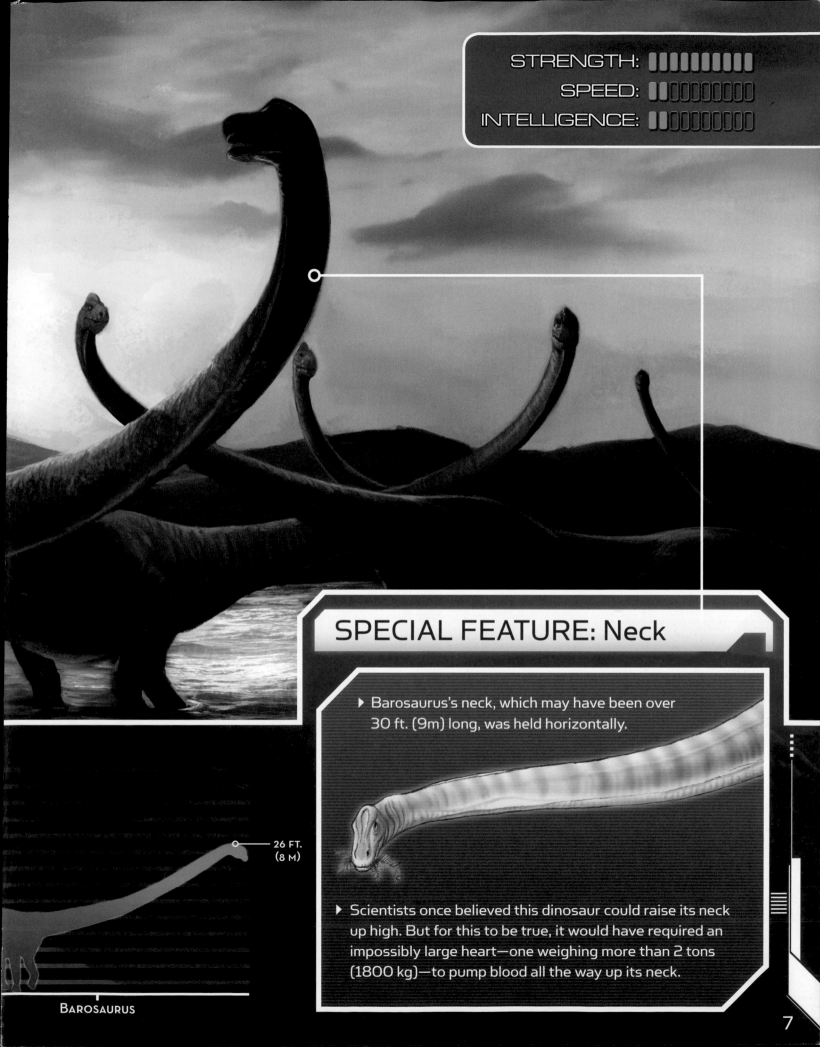

SPECIAL FEATURE: Neck

▸ Barosaurus's neck, which may have been over 30 ft. (9m) long, was held horizontally.

▸ Scientists once believed this dinosaur could raise its neck up high. But for this to be true, it would have required an impossibly large heart—one weighing more than 2 tons (1800 kg)—to pump blood all the way up its neck.

26 FT.
(8 M)

BAROSAURUS

BARYONYX

(BEAR-ee-ON-iks) "Heavy claw"

After its frighteningly sharp thumb claw was excavated, the media nicknamed Baryonyx "Claws"—a reference to the horror film _Jaws_.

QUICK FACTS

▸ Baryonyx may have used its short yet powerful arms to tackle and hold the slippery fish it fed on.

▸ Perhaps Baryonyx fished the way bears do: snapping their jaws on fish, and also swatting them out of the water with their front feet.

Curved claws

SPECIAL FEATURE: Snout

▸ Unlike most carnivores, Baryonyx didn't have razor-sharp teeth. Instead, its snout was lined with cone-shaped teeth.

▸ The bulbous tip of its snout held a clump of teeth—much like the snouts of fish-eating crocodiles today.

▸ Baryonyx used its snout to feed on fish, as well as young dinosaurs.

DINO-SIZE

Baryonyx was twice the size of a large crocodile.

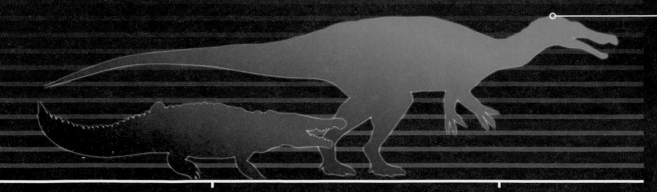

9 FT.
(2.7 M)

CROCODILE

BARYONYX

STRENGTH: ||||||||☐☐☐
SPEED: |||||||☐☐☐☐
INTELLIGENCE: ||||||||☐☐☐

VITAL STATS

LENGTH: 30 FT. (9 M)
WEIGHT: 4,000 LBS. (1,800 KG)
PERIOD: EARLY CRETACEOUS
PLACE: ENGLAND, NORTHERN
SPAIN, PORTUGAL

[CARCHARODONTOSAURUS]

(car-CARE-uh-DON-tuh-SOR-us) "Shark-toothed lizard"

Carcharadontosaurus had large sharklike teeth, which inspired German paleontologist Ernst Stromer von Reichenbach to name the creature after *Carcharadon carcharias*, the great white shark.

VITAL STATS

LENGTH: ABOUT 45 FT. (14 M)
WEIGHT: 6,400 LBS. (2,900 KG)
PERIOD: MIDDLE CRETACEOUS
PLACE: NORTH AFRICA

QUICK FACTS

▶ Carcharadontosaurus remains are rare. Important fossils were discovered in the 1930s, but were destroyed during a World War II bombing.

▶ Although its skull was more than 5 ft. (1.5 m) long, its brain might have been only about 8 in. (20 cm) long and 1.5 in. (3.8 cm) wide.

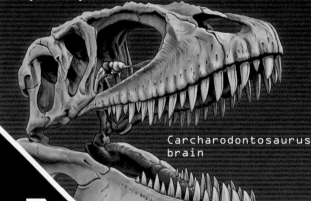

Carcharodontosaurus brain

DINO-SIZE

Carcharadontosaurus was about as tall as a double-decker bus.

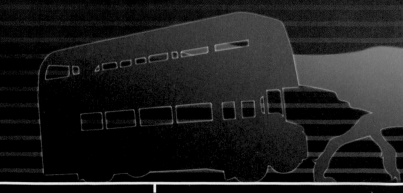

DOUBLE-DECKER BUS

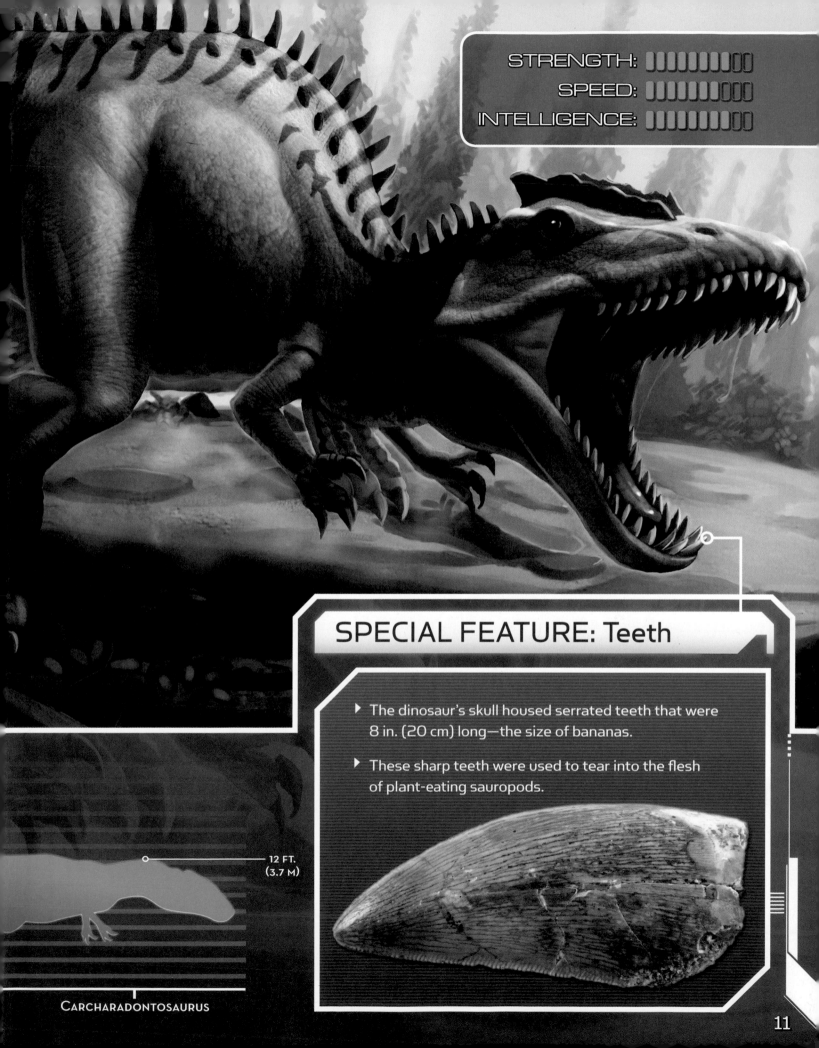

SPECIAL FEATURE: Teeth

▶ The dinosaur's skull housed serrated teeth that were 8 in. (20 cm) long—the size of bananas.

▶ These sharp teeth were used to tear into the flesh of plant-eating sauropods.

12 FT.
(3.7 M)

CARCHARADONTOSAURUS

11

CARNOTAURUS

(CAR-nuh-TOR-us) "Flesh-eating bull"

With horns on its head and a short powerful neck, Carnotaurus resembled a bull in some ways.

Vital Stats

Length: About 25 ft. (7.5 m)
Weight: 2,000 lbs. (900 kg)
Period: Early Cretaceous
Place: Argentina

Quick Facts

▶ Carnotaurus's forelimbs were so short that neither hand could touch the other.

▶ Unlike most other dinosaurs, which had sideways-facing eyes, Carnotaurus had eyes that faced almost forward. This may have helped the dinosaur focus better on its prey.

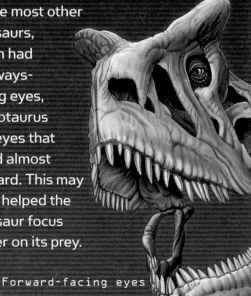

Forward-facing eyes

Dino-Size

Carnotaurus was about the height of an African elephant.

African Elephant

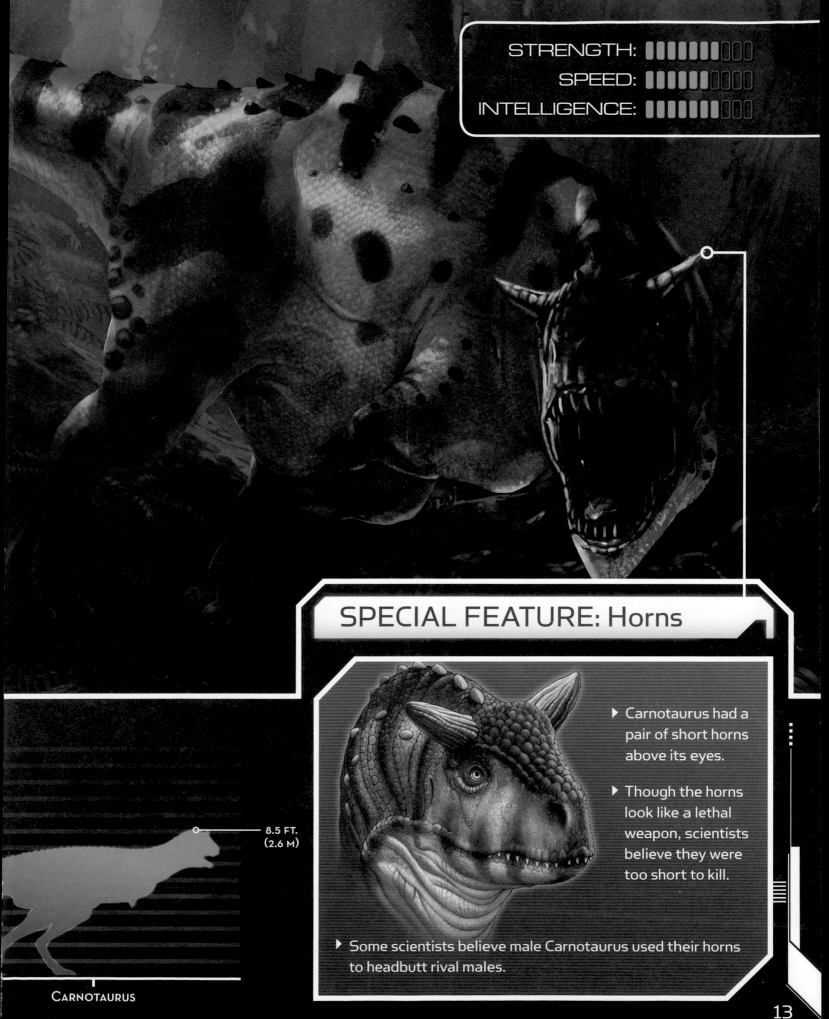

SPECIAL FEATURE: Horns

▶ Carnotaurus had a pair of short horns above its eyes.

▶ Though the horns look like a lethal weapon, scientists believe they were too short to kill.

▶ Some scientists believe male Carnotaurus used their horns to headbutt rival males.

8.5 FT.
(2.6 M)

CARNOTAURUS

13

[COELOPHYSIS]

(SEE-lo-FI-sis) "Hollow form"

Coelophysis had hollow limb bones, much like birds today.

Quick Facts

▶ Its hollow leg bones reduced Coelophysis's total body weight, which may have allowed the dinosaur to move fast.

▶ In 1998, astronauts traveling aboard Space Shuttle *Endeavor* packed a Coelophysis skull along, just for fun. They transferred the skull to the space station Mir and then brought it back to Earth.

Hollow leg bone

SPECIAL FEATURE:
Ghost Ranch Mystery

▶ In 1947, hundreds of Coelophysis skeletons were discovered at Ghost Ranch, New Mexico. The dinosaurs may have died together in a catastrophic event, such as a flood. Scientists say these dinosaurs were either hunting together, or had gathered around a watering hole.

▶ A small Coelophysis lodged inside a larger one was also discovered at the site. Originally, scientists thought one Coelophysis had eaten the other. It was later shown that the larger specimen had collapsed on top of the smaller one.

Dino-Size

Coelophysis was about the length of a male polar bear.

3.5 FT.
(1 M)

POLAR BEAR   COELOPHYSIS

COMPSOGNATHUS

(COMP-SOG-NAY-THUS) "ELEGANT JAW"

Compsognathus had several remarkable features, including its delicate jaw. It may also have had hairlike feathers.

QUICK FACTS

▶ Compsognathus was a carnivorous dinosaur. Its diet included small lizards, such as Bavarisaurus.

▶ Compsognathus's "elegant jaw" consisted of an upper jaw made from long, slender struts of interlocking bones that rested on top of a shallow lower jaw.

Modern lizard resembling Bavarisaurus

SPECIAL FEATURE: Locomotion

▶ Studies show that the bipedal Compsognathus could reach speeds of 40 mph (64 kph). That's faster than the fastest living animal on two legs, the ostrich.

▶ Compsognathus was built for speed: Its rear legs were slim, with short thighs and shins, and its feet were very long.

▶ Compsognathus used its tail for balance as it ran and turned.

DINO-SIZE

Compsognathus was roughly the length of a domestic cat.

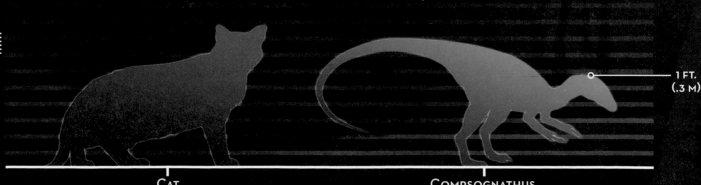

1 FT.
(.3 M)

CAT   COMPSOGNATHUS

STRENGTH: ▌▌□□□□□□□□
SPEED: ▌▌▌▌▌▌▌▌□□
INTELLIGENCE: ▌▌▌▌▌▌□□□□

Vital Stats

Length: About 3.5 ft. (1 m)
Weight: About 7 lbs. (3 kg)
Period: Late Jurassic
Place: Germany, France

[DEINONYCHUS]

(DIE-NON-ih-cuss) "Terrible claw"

Deinonychus was small but powerful, and because of its large sharp claws, it was able to kill creatures larger than itself.

Quick Facts

▶ In proportion to its body size, the brain of Deinonychus was the biggest of any reptile that ever lived.

▶ Recent studies indicate the dinosaur was able to use its forelegs to clutch objects to its chest.

▶ Deinonychus may have hunted in packs.

SPECIAL FEATURE: Claw

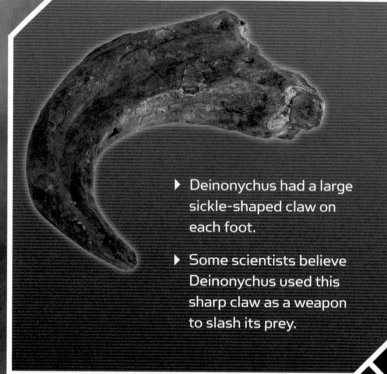

▶ Deinonychus had a large sickle-shaped claw on each foot.

▶ Some scientists believe Deinonychus used this sharp claw as a weapon to slash its prey.

Dino-Size

Deinonychus was slightly longer than a male Bengal tiger.

3 FT.
(.9 M)

BENGAL TIGER   DEINONYCHUS

STRENGTH: ‖‖‖‖‖‖‖‖□□□
SPEED: ‖‖‖‖‖‖‖‖‖□□
INTELLIGENCE: ‖‖‖‖‖‖‖‖‖□

VITAL STATS

LENGTH: ABOUT 11 FT. (3 M)
WEIGHT: 160 LBS. (73 KG)
PERIOD: EARLY CRETACEOUS
PLACE: WESTERN UNITED STATES

DIPLODOCUS

(DIP-LOD-UH-CUSS) "DOUBLE BEAM"

With its sturdy legs and long neck and tail, Diplodocus is often compared to a suspension bridge.

VITAL STATS

LENGTH: UP TO 110 FT. (34 M)
WEIGHT: UP TO 30,000 LBS.
(13,600 KG)
PERIOD: LATE JURASSIC
PLACE: WESTERN
NORTH AMERICA

QUICK FACTS

▸ Diplodocus's neck may have been 20 ft. (6 m) long.

▸ This plant-eater had no teeth in the back of its mouth for chewing.

Diplodocus skull

DINO-SIZE

Diplodocus was about the length of three school buses!

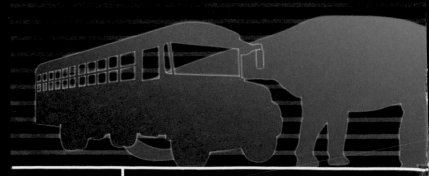

SCHOOL BUS

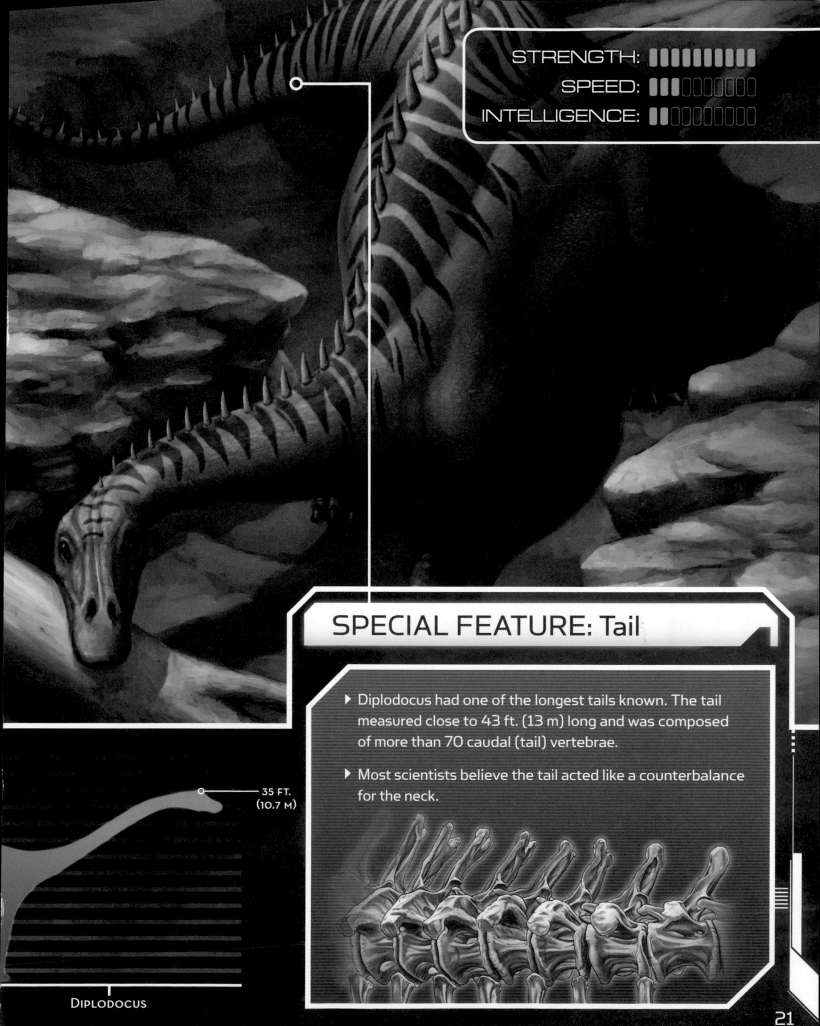

SPECIAL FEATURE: Tail

▶ Diplodocus had one of the longest tails known. The tail measured close to 43 ft. (13 m) long and was composed of more than 70 caudal (tail) vertebrae.

▶ Most scientists believe the tail acted like a counterbalance for the neck.

35 FT.
(10.7 M)

DIPLODOCUS

DROMICEIOMIMUS

(DROH-MEE-SEE-OH-MY-MUS) "EMU MIMIC"

With its long limbs, large eyes, and toothless beak, Dromiceiomimus resembled a large bird, such as an emu or ostrich.

VITAL STATS

LENGTH: 12 FT. (3.7 M)
WEIGHT: UP TO 330 LBS. (150 KG)
PERIOD: LATE CRETACEOUS
PLACE: ALBERTA, CANADA

QUICK FACTS

▶ Dromiceiomimus was a fast sprinter, and could have exceeded 38 mph (61 kph).

▶ Because Dromiceiomimus had a wide pelvis, scientists believe this dinosaur could have given birth to live young. However, it might be more likely that Dromiceiomimus laid very large eggs, much like ostriches do today.

DINO-SIZE

This birdlike dinosaur would have been about the length of a Pacific walrus.

WALRUS

SPECIAL FEATURE: Eyes

▶ Dromiceiomimus had unusually large eyes. Its eye sockets measured 3 in. (7.6 cm) in diameter. That's larger than the diameter of a tennis ball.

▶ Because of its large eyes, scientists believe Dromiceiomimus might have been nocturnal, or active at night.

5.5 FT. (1.7 M)

DROMICEIOMIMUS

EUOPLOCEPHALUS

(YOO-oh-pluh-SEF-uh-lus) "Well-armored head"

Euoplocephalus's heavily armored body would have been a challenge for any predator to penetrate.

VITAL STATS

Length: 20 ft. (6 m)
Weight: 4,400 lbs. (2,000 kg)
Time: Late Cretaceous
Place: Alberta, Canada, and Montana

QUICK FACTS

▸ Euoplocephalus had small leaf-shaped teeth, which it used to graze on low-lying plants.

▸ At the end of its rigid tail was a bony club, which acted like a wrecking ball. When attacked, Euoplocephalus could swing this club at an enemy with bone-crushing results.

Bony club

DINO-SIZE

Euoplocephalus was about the length of an Indian elephant.

Indian Elephant

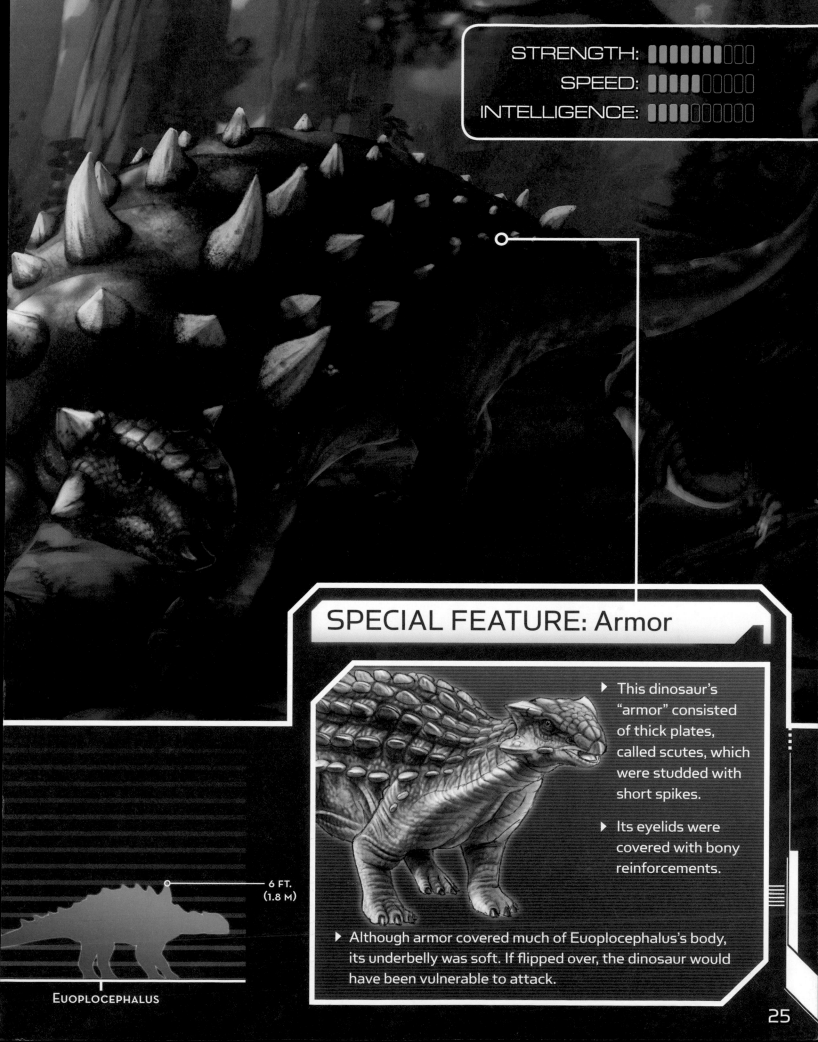

STRENGTH: ▐▐▐▐▐▐▐☐☐☐
SPEED: ▐▐▐▐▐☐☐☐☐☐
INTELLIGENCE: ▐▐▐▐☐☐☐☐☐☐

SPECIAL FEATURE: Armor

▶ This dinosaur's "armor" consisted of thick plates, called scutes, which were studded with short spikes.

▶ Its eyelids were covered with bony reinforcements.

▶ Although armor covered much of Euoplocephalus's body, its underbelly was soft. If flipped over, the dinosaur would have been vulnerable to attack.

6 FT.
(1.8 M)

EUOPLOCEPHALUS

GALLIMIMUS

(GAL-uh-MY-muss) "Chicken mimic"

Its small head, large eyes, and long legs gave this "chicken mimic" more of an ostrichlike appearance.

Vital Stats

Length: 20 ft. (6 m)
Weight: 970 lbs. (440 kg)
Period: Late Cretaceous
Place: Mongolia

Quick Facts

▸ Gallimimus may have fed on insects, small vertebrates, eggs, and plants.

▸ It had small shovel-like hands, which it may have used to dig for food.

▸ Gallimius's light, streamlined body allowed the dinosaur to run as fast as 40 mph (64 kph).

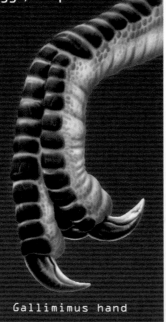

Gallimimus hand

Dino-Size

The ostrichlike Gallimimus was actually much bigger than an ostrich.

Ostrich

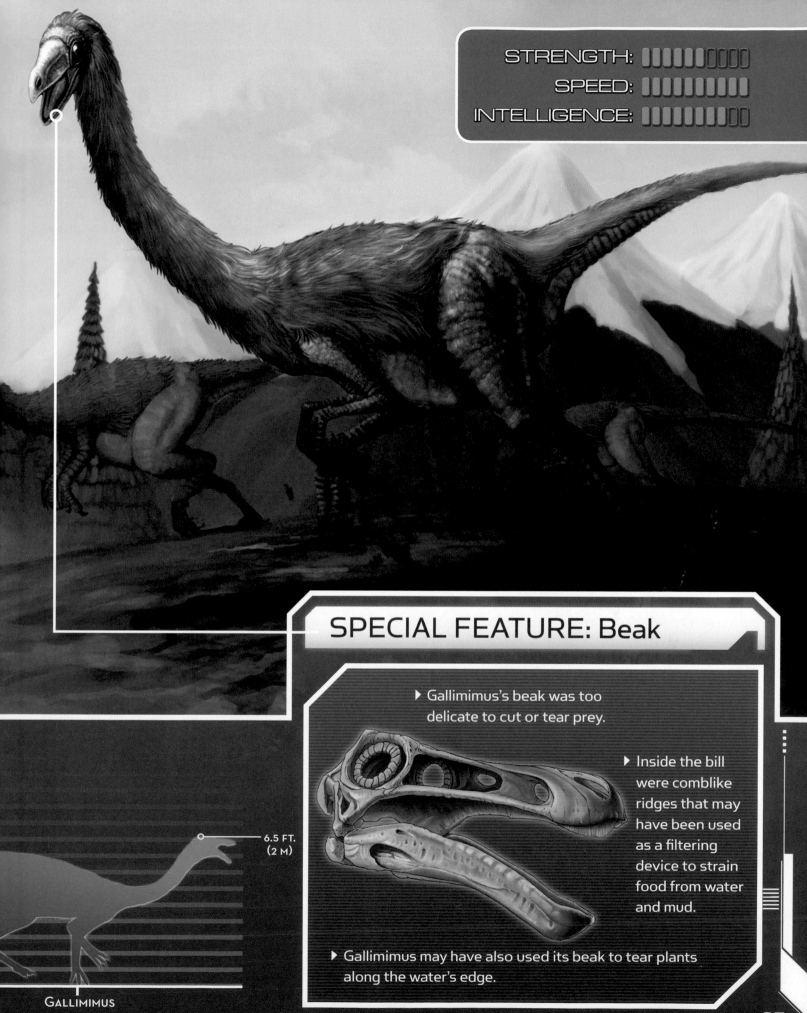

6.5 FT.
(2 M)

GALLIMIMUS

SPECIAL FEATURE: Beak

▶ Gallimimus's beak was too delicate to cut or tear prey.

▶ Inside the bill were comblike ridges that may have been used as a filtering device to strain food from water and mud.

▶ Gallimimus may have also used its beak to tear plants along the water's edge.

HETERODONTOSAURUS

(HET-uh-roh-DON-tuh-SOR-us) "DIFFERENT-TOOTHED LIZARD"

Unlike most dinosaurs, which had one type of tooth, Heterodontosaurus had three types.

VITAL STATS

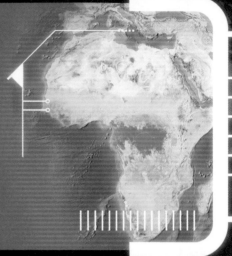

LENGTH: 3 FT. (.9 M)
WEIGHT: AT LEAST 6 LBS. (2.7 KG)
PERIOD: EARLY JURASSIC
PLACE: SOUTH AFRICA

QUICK FACTS

▸ One particular juvenile Heterodontosaurus is thought to have weighed only ²⁄₅ lb. (.2 kg).

▸ Heterodontosaurus had one opposable finger on each hand. Opposable fingers can bend to touch the other digits on the same hand. This would have helped the dinosaur grasp food.

DINO-SIZE

Heterodontosaurus was about the size of a wild turkey.

TURKEY

SPECIAL FEATURE: Tusks

▸ In the front of its jaw were small teeth that may have been used for chopping plants.

▸ Next was a pair of tusks that may have been used in courtship displays.

▸ The third type of tooth—tall and squared off—may have been used for chewing.

1 FT.
(.3 M)

HETERODONTOSAURUS

[HYPSILOPHODON]

(hip-sih-LOAF-uh-don) "High-crested tooth"

Hypsilophodon was known for its tall, ridged teeth, which it used to feed on low-lying vegetation.

Quick Facts

▸ Scientists once believed that Hypsilophodon lived in trees. However, later studies show it was a fast sprinter that stayed on the ground.

▸ The tendons, or tissues connecting muscles to bone, in the dinosaur's tail were bony. This stiffened the tail and helped keep it off the ground while the dinosaur was running.

SPECIAL FEATURE: Teeth

▸ Hypsilophodon's teeth were set far back in its jaw. This suggests that the dinosaur had cheeks.

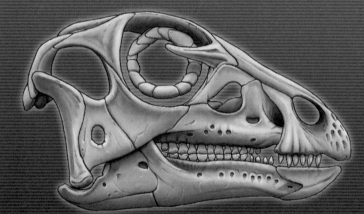

▸ When Hypsilophodon closed its beak, the teeth in the upper jaw slid down against the outer part of the teeth in the lower jaw. This rubbing action kept its teeth sharp.

Dino-Size

Hypsilophodon was about the length of a caribou.

2.5 FT.
(.8 M)

CARIBOU   HYPSILOPHODON

STRENGTH: ▐▐▐▐□□□□□□
SPEED: ▐▐▐▐▐▐▐▐▐□
INTELLIGENCE: ▐▐▐▐▐□□□□□

Vital Stats

Length: About 7 ft. (2 m)
Weight: Up to 150 lbs. (68 kg)
Period: Early Cretaceous
Place: England, Portugal, Spain, and South Dakota

LIOPLEURODON
(LIE-oh-PLUR-uh-don) "Smooth-sided tooth"

Liopleurodon's supersharp teeth had smooth sides, a feature that gave this marine reptile its name.

Vital Stats

LENGTH: 33–65 FT. (10–20 M); THIS IS STILL BEING DEBATED.
WEIGHT: UNKNOWN
PERIOD: MIDDLE TO LATE JURASSIC
PLACE: ENGLAND, FRANCE, RUSSIA, AND GERMANY

Quick Facts

▸ This fierce marine predator, not actually a dinosaur, was one of the largest carnivores that ever lived.

▸ The name Liopleurodon was created on the basis of the first fossils that were discovered from the reptile: three teeth found in different sites in Europe.

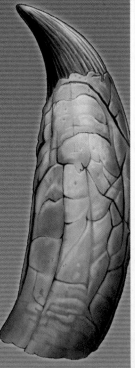

Dino-Size

Liopleurodon was probably at least twice as long as a great white shark.

GREAT WHITE

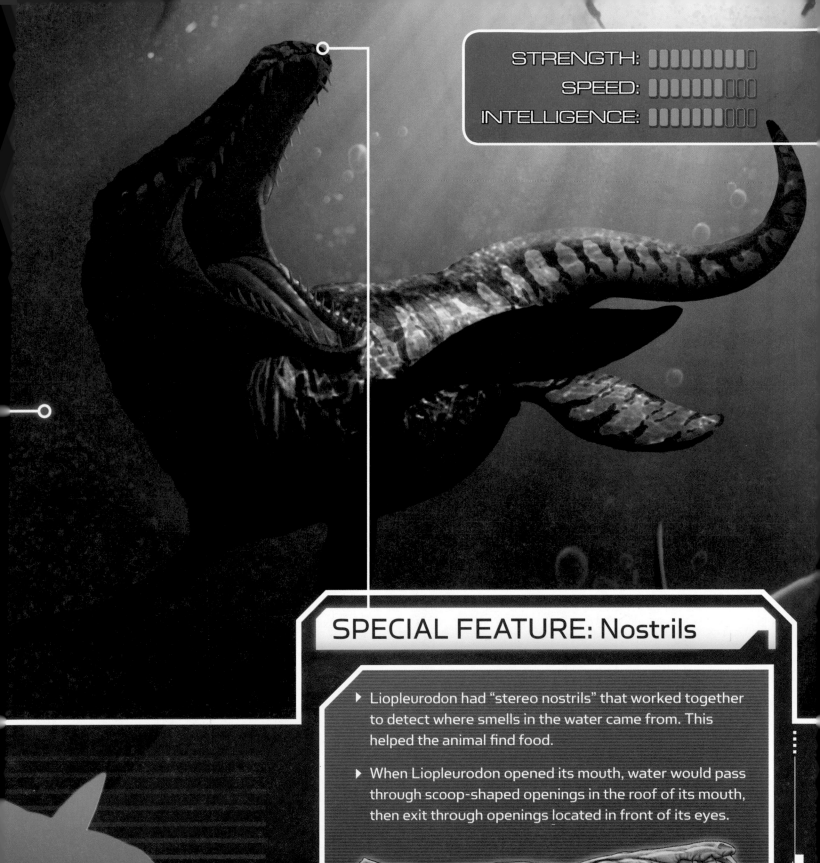

STRENGTH: ⬛⬛⬛⬛⬛⬛⬛⬛⬛⬜
SPEED: ⬛⬛⬛⬛⬛⬛⬛⬜⬜⬜
INTELLIGENCE: ⬛⬛⬛⬛⬛⬛⬛⬜⬜⬜

SPECIAL FEATURE: Nostrils

▶ Liopleurodon had "stereo nostrils" that worked together to detect where smells in the water came from. This helped the animal find food.

▶ When Liopleurodon opened its mouth, water would pass through scoop-shaped openings in the roof of its mouth, then exit through openings located in front of its eyes.

LIOPLEURODON
33–65 FT. (10-20 M) LONG

MAIASAURA

(MY-uh-SOR-uh) "CARING MOTHER LIZARD"

Maiasaura was a caring parent that looked after its babies and brought food back to its nest.

VITAL STATS

LENGTH: UP TO 30 FT. (9 M)
WEIGHT: UP TO 8,000 LBS. (3,630 KG)
PERIOD: LATE CRETACEOUS
PLACE: MONTANA

QUICK FACTS

▸ The mouth of Maiasaura was wide at the front, much like a duck's bill. Maiasaura lived in large herds that may have consisted of 10,000 other Maiasaura dinosaurs.

▸ Maiasaura hatchlings were up to 16 in. (41 cm) long, and could grow to 10 ft. (3 m) in just one year!

DINO-SIZE

Maiasaura was almost four times as long as a lioness.

LIONESS

6.5 FT.
(2 M)

MAIASAURA

SPECIAL FEATURE: Nesting

▸ Maiasaura could lay more than 20 eggs—about the size of grapefruits—in one breeding cycle.

▸ The nests were holes scooped out of the ground.

▸ Instead of incubating their eggs by sitting on them, Maiasaura kept its eggs warm by placing vegetation inside the nest.

MUTTABURRASAURUS

(MUTT-UH-BURR-UH-SOR-US) "LIZARD FROM MUTTABURRA"

Muttaburrasaurus—a dinosaur that roamed Australia over 97 million years ago—gets its name from Muttaburra, an area in Queensland where it was first discovered.

QUICK FACTS

▸ Although Muttaburrasaurus spent most of its time walking on four legs, it was capable of stretching upward on its hind legs.

▸ Muttaburrasaurus might have had hooflike pads on its forelimbs, with each pad formed of three middle digits joined together.

▸ Muttaburrasaurus used its large, hollow muzzle to produce calls.

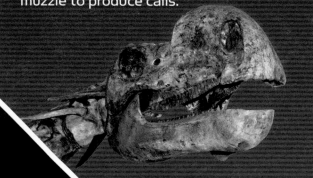

SPECIAL FEATURE: Habitat

▸ Muttaburrasaurus lived in open woodlands that covered large areas of Australia more than 100 million years ago.

▸ The forest was rich with plants, such as ferns and cycads, which would have provided Muttaburrasaurus with food.

DINO-SIZE

Muttaburrasaurus was twice the length of a hippopotamus.

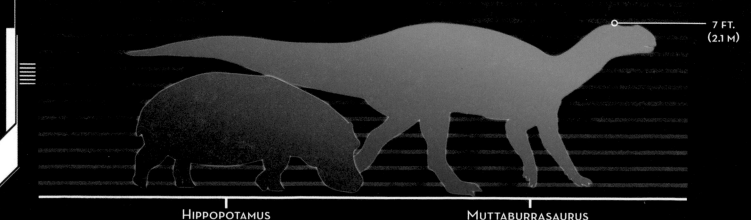

7 FT.
(2.1 M)

HIPPOPOTAMUS   MUTTABURRASAURUS

STRENGTH: ▮▮▮▮▮▮▮▯▯▯
SPEED: ▮▮▮▮▮▮▯▯▯▯
INTELLIGENCE: ▮▮▮▮▮▯▯▯▯▯

VITAL STATS

LENGTH: 23 FT. (7 M)
WEIGHT: UP TO 8,000 LBS.
(3,630 KG)
PERIOD: EARLY CRETACEOUS
PLACE: AUSTRALIA

OVIRAPTOR

(OH-vih-RAP-tor) "Egg thief"

Scientists once thought that Oviraptor stole and devoured the eggs of other dinosaurs. Now, they believe it was a case of mistaken identity.

QUICK FACTS

▶ Oviraptor had long hind legs with sharp claws on each foot.

▶ Most Oviraptor skulls that have been discovered have a striking feature: a large crest just above the eyes.

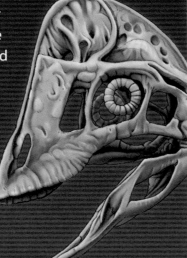

SPECIAL FEATURE: Bad Reputation

▶ When scientists discovered an Oviraptor skull alongside a nest of what they believed were Protoceratops eggs, they assumed Oviraptor died trying to steal the eggs.

▶ Recent finds have proved that the eggs did not belong to Protoceratops. The eggs had actually been laid by the Oviraptor—making the accused "egg thief" a parent, not a thief.

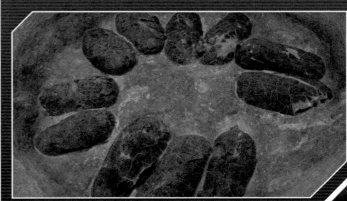

DINO-SIZE

Oviraptor was about the size of an emu.

5 FT.
(1.5 M)

EMU   OVIRAPTOR

STRENGTH: ▌▌▌▌▌□□□□□
SPEED: ▌▌▌▌▌▌▌▌▌▌
INTELLIGENCE: ▌▌▌▌▌▌▌▌▌▌

VITAL STATS

LENGTH: 8 FT. (2.4 M)
WEIGHT: UP TO 76 LBS. (34 KG)
PERIOD: LATE CRETACEOUS
PLACE: MONGOLIA

PACHYCEPHALOSAURUS

(PACK-EE-SEFF-A-LOH-SOR-US) "THICK-HEADED LIZARD"

Pachycephalosaurus is famous for the large thick dome on top of its skull.

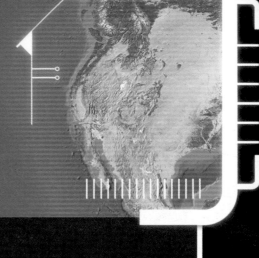

VITAL STATS

LENGTH: 15 FT. (4.6 M)
WEIGHT: 1,100 LBS. (500 KG)
PERIOD: LATE CRETACEOUS
PLACE: MONTANA, SOUTH DAKOTA, WYOMING

QUICK FACTS

▸ Pachycephalosaurus is believed to have had binocular vision. That means it could judge how far away objects were.

▸ This plant-eater had a muzzle ending in a pointed beak.

DINO-SIZE

Scientists estimate that Pachycephalosaurus could have been as long as a large car.

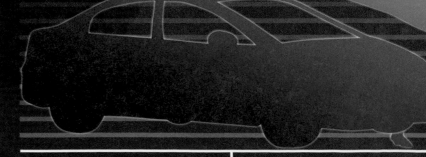

CAR

STRENGTH: ■■■■■□□□□□
SPEED: ■■■■□□□□□□
INTELLIGENCE: ■■■■■□□□□□

SPECIAL FEATURE: Dome Skull

▸ The bony dome on top of Pachycephalosaurus's head was up to 9 in. (23 cm) thick.

▸ Scientist believe the dome was used for flank-butting. The dinosaur would bend its head downward and strike a rival Pachycephalosaurus on its side.

5.5 FT.
(1.7 M)

PACHYCEPHALOSAURUS

41

PARASAUROLOPHUS

(PAIR-A-SOR-OLL-UH-FUSS) "LIKE SAUROLOPHUS (CRESTED LIZARD)"

Parasaurolophus is well known for the hollow curved crest that swept back over its neck from the top of its head.

VITAL STATS

LENGTH: 30 FT. (9 M)
WEIGHT: 5,400 LBS. (2,450 KG)
PERIOD: LATE CRETACEOUS
PLACE: NEW MEXICO, UTAH, AND ALBERTA, CANADA

QUICK FACTS

▸ Parasaurolophus belonged to a family of dinosaurs called hadrosaurids, which were known for their "duck bills" and the unusual crests on their heads.

▸ Parasaurolophus ran on two legs, but it likely foraged for plants on all fours.

DINO-SIZE

Parasaurolophus was three times the length of a Komodo dragon, the world's largest lizard.

KOMODO DRAGON

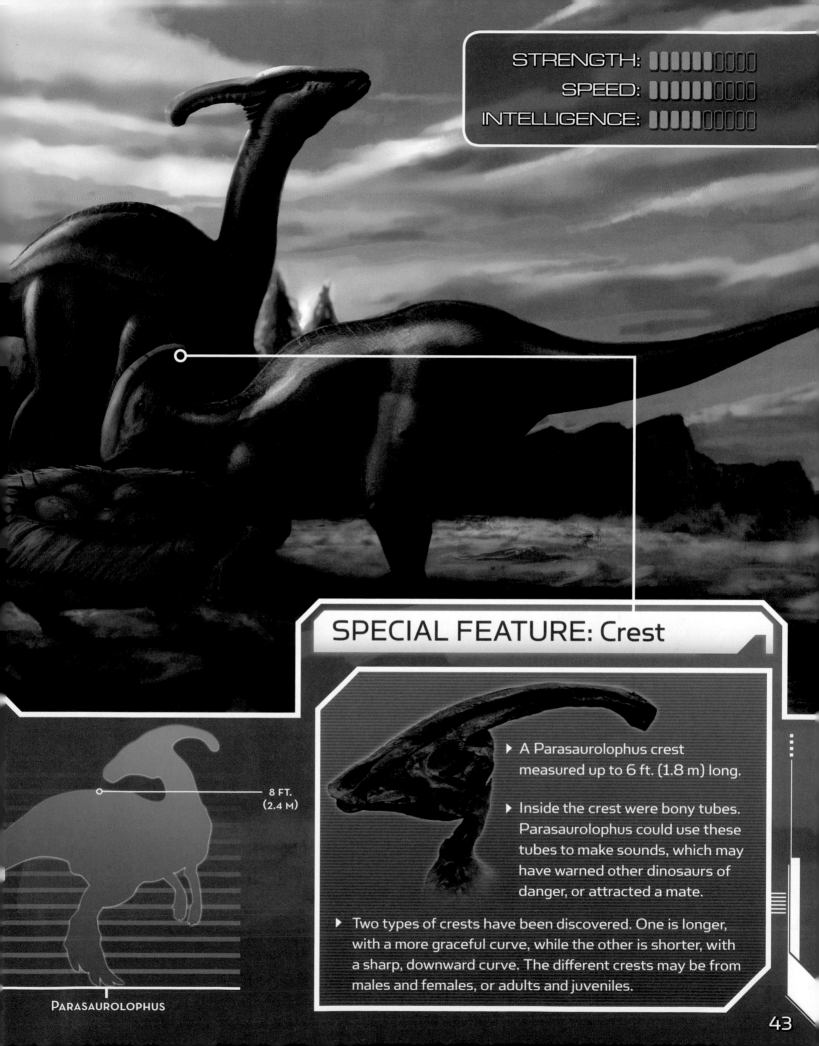

STRENGTH: ⬛⬛⬛⬛⬛⬛⬜⬜⬜⬜
SPEED: ⬛⬛⬛⬛⬛⬛⬜⬜⬜⬜
INTELLIGENCE: ⬛⬛⬛⬛⬛⬜⬜⬜⬜⬜

SPECIAL FEATURE: Crest

▶ A Parasaurolophus crest measured up to 6 ft. (1.8 m) long.

▶ Inside the crest were bony tubes. Parasaurolophus could use these tubes to make sounds, which may have warned other dinosaurs of danger, or attracted a mate.

▶ Two types of crests have been discovered. One is longer, with a more graceful curve, while the other is shorter, with a sharp, downward curve. The different crests may be from males and females, or adults and juveniles.

8 FT. (2.4 M)

PARASAUROLOPHUS

43

PTERANODON

(ter-RAN-uh-don) "WINGED AND TOOTHLESS"

Pteranodon was not a dinosaur, but a winged reptile that soared through prehistoric skies.

QUICK FACTS

▶ Pteranodon had no teeth—it swallowed meals whole.

▶ Pteranodons and related animals had bony crests on their heads. Males may have used them to attract mates.

Dsungaripterus

Tapejara

Nyctosaurus

SPECIAL FEATURE: Wings

Structure of Pteranodon's wing

▶ Pteranodon had three clawed fingers and an elongated fourth finger that formed the structure of its wing.

▶ It's likely that Pteranodon had a stretchy membrane attached to its wing bones—like modern bats.

▶ Pteranodon used its large wings to glide on rising air currents, called thermals. This helped Pteranodon generate lift and soar.

DINO-SIZE

Pteranodon's wingspan measured about 30 ft. (9 m). That's almost three times the length of the wingspan of an albatross, the living bird with the largest wingspan.

ALBATROSS

PTERANODON
6 FT. (1.8 M) LONG, FROM NOSE TO TAIL

Vital Stats

Length: 6 ft. (1.8 m)
Weight: 40 lbs. (18 kg)
Period: Late Cretaceous
Place: Mainly midwestern and southwestern United States

STRENGTH: ▮▮▮▮▮▯▯▯▯▯
SPEED: ▮▮▮▮▮▮▮▮▯▯
INTELLIGENCE: ▮▮▮▮▮▮▮▯▯▯

SCUTELLOSAURUS

(SKOO-TELL-UH-SOR-US) "LITTLE SHIELD LIZARD"

Although small, Scutellosaurus wasn't defenseless—it had a shield of armor for protection.

VITAL STATS

LENGTH: 4 FT. (1.2 M)
WEIGHT: 22 LBS. (10 KG)
PERIOD: EARLY JURASSIC
PLACE: ARIZONA

QUICK FACTS

▸ Scutellosaurus belonged to an order of dinosaurs called ornithischians, which were beaked plant-eaters with hipbones similar to those of birds.

▸ Scutellosaurus had two types of teeth, incisors and leaf-shaped cheek teeth, which it used to feed on vegetation.

Leaf-shaped cheek teeth

DINO-SIZE

Scutellosaurus was much smaller than a gray wolf.

GRAY WOLF

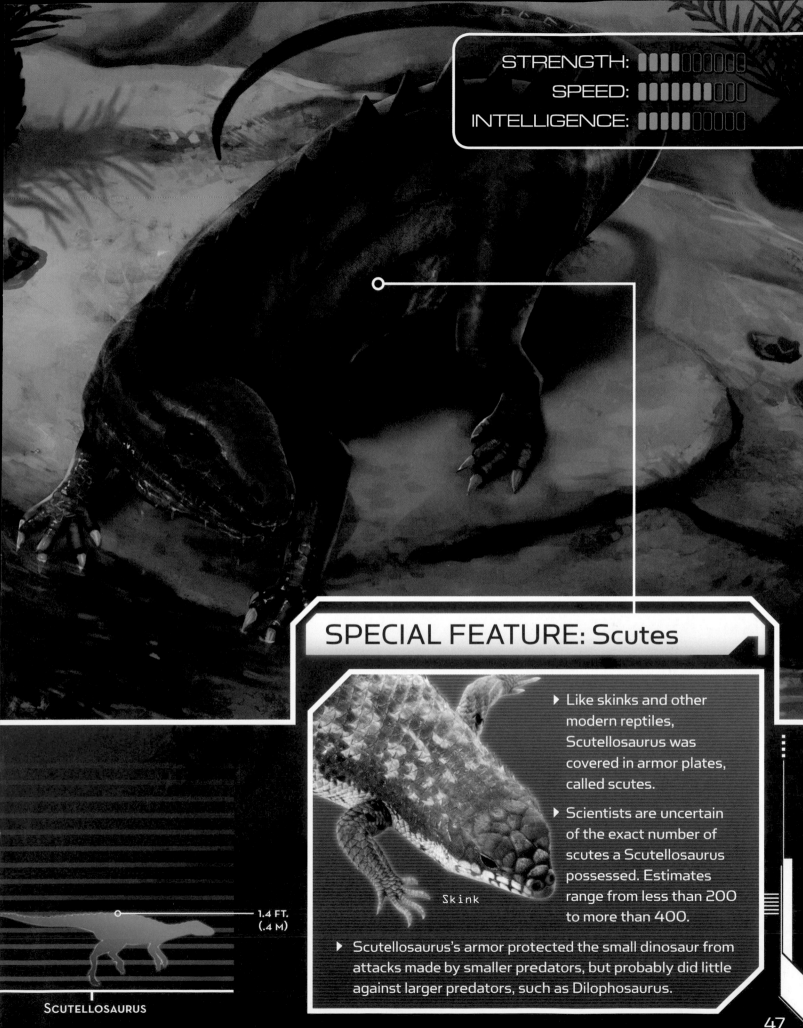

STRENGTH: ▮▮▮▮☐☐☐☐☐☐☐
SPEED: ▮▮▮▮▮▮▮▮☐☐☐
INTELLIGENCE: ▮▮▮▮▮▮☐☐☐☐☐

SPECIAL FEATURE: Scutes

Skink

▶ Like skinks and other modern reptiles, Scutellosaurus was covered in armor plates, called scutes.

▶ Scientists are uncertain of the exact number of scutes a Scutellosaurus possessed. Estimates range from less than 200 to more than 400.

▶ Scutellosaurus's armor protected the small dinosaur from attacks made by smaller predators, but probably did little against larger predators, such as Dilophosaurus.

1.4 FT.
(.4 M)

SCUTELLOSAURUS

SEISMOSAURUS

(SIZE-mo-SOR-us) "Earthquake lizard"

Seismosaurus was so large that when it walked, it may have caused the ground to shake!

VITAL STATS

LENGTH: MORE THAN 130 FT.
(40 M)
WEIGHT: 80,000 LBS.
(36,300 KG)
PERIOD: LATE JURASSIC
PLACE: NEW MEXICO

QUICK FACTS

▶ Scientists discovered a Seismosaurus skeleton in 1985. It was so firmly buried in rock that it took them eight years to dig it out.

▶ Seismosaurus may have swept its long neck from side to side along the ground, looking for low-lying plants to eat.

DINO-SIZE

Seismosaurus was longer than a Boeing 737!

737

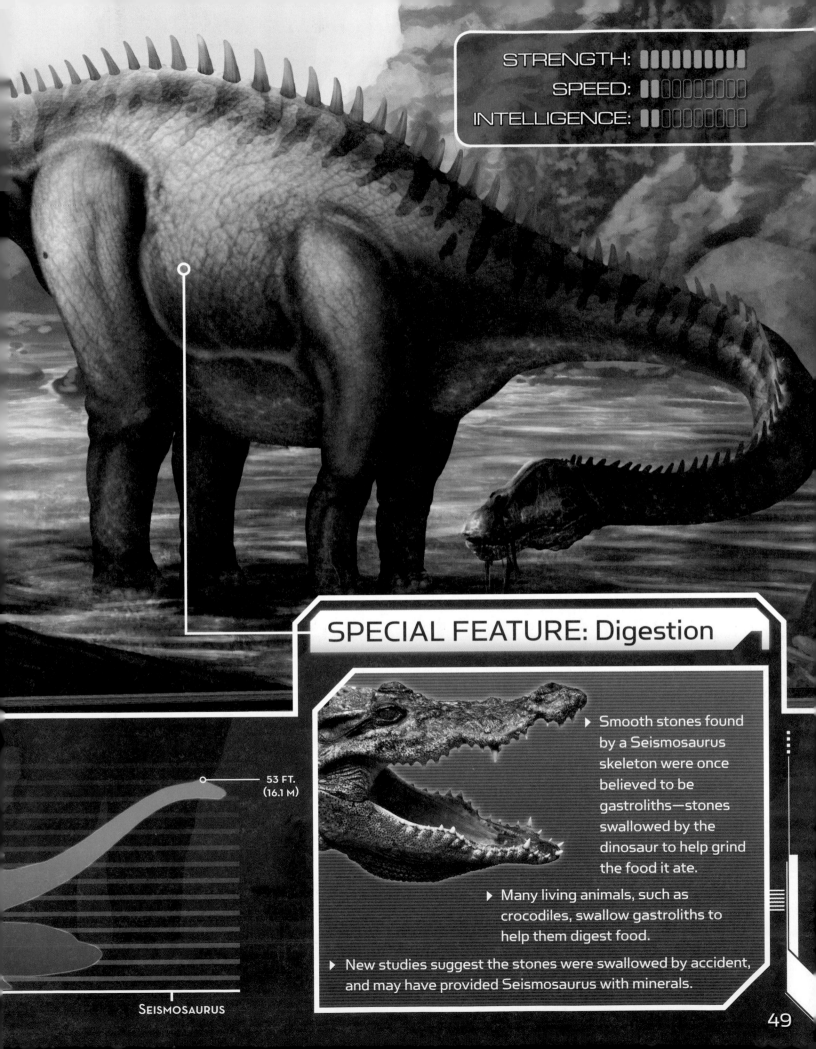

STRENGTH: ▮▮▮▮▮▮▮▮▮▮
SPEED: ▮▮□□□□□□□□
INTELLIGENCE: ▮▮□□□□□□□□

53 FT.
(16.1 M)

SEISMOSAURUS

SPECIAL FEATURE: Digestion

▶ Smooth stones found by a Seismosaurus skeleton were once believed to be gastroliths—stones swallowed by the dinosaur to help grind the food it ate.

▶ Many living animals, such as crocodiles, swallow gastroliths to help them digest food.

▶ New studies suggest the stones were swallowed by accident, and may have provided Seismosaurus with minerals.

SPINOSAURUS

(SPY-no-SOR-uhss) "Spine lizard"

With a "sail" of spines raised high along its back, Spinosaurus was an intimidating dinosaur.

VITAL STATS

LENGTH: 50 FT. (15 M)
WEIGHT: 19,800 LBS. (9,000 KG)
PERIOD: MIDDLE CRETACEOUS
PLACE: NORTH AFRICA

QUICK FACTS

▸ Most meat-eating dinosaurs had curved teeth. But Spinosaurus had straight, sharp teeth, which it used to skewer the flesh of prey.

▸ A recently discovered pterosaur fossil contained a Spinosaurus tooth stuck in its spine. The find suggests that Spinosaurus fed on these winged reptiles.

DINO-SIZE

Spinosaurus was almost twice as long as a San Francisco cable car.

CABLE CAR

SPECIAL FEATURE: Sail

▸ Spinosaurus had a sail-like structure on its back. This sail was made of skin-covered spines.

  ▸ The sail may have been used to regulate the dinosaur's body temperature, or to attract mates during courtship.

    ▸ At its highest point, the sail measured 6.5 ft. (2 m) above the backbone.

20 FT.
(6 M)

SPINOSAURUS

STEGOSAURUS

(STEG-UH-SOR-US) "ROOF LIZARD"

Stegosaurus's armored plates stood upright on its back. Scientists are still debating how the plates were arranged.

VITAL STATS

LENGTH: 30 FT. (9 M)
WEIGHT: 6,600 LBS. (3,000 KG)
PERIOD: LATE JURASSIC
PLACE: WESTERN NORTH AMERICA, WESTERN EUROPE, SOUTHERN INDIA, CHINA, AND SOUTHERN AFRICA

QUICK FACTS

▶ It was once believed that Stegosaurus had a second brain in its tail. Scientists now know this isn't true.

▶ The tail featured four spikes that were 2–3 ft. (.6–1 m) long. The spikes were most likely used in combat.

DINO-SIZE

Stegosaurus was about the size of a city bus.

CITY BUS

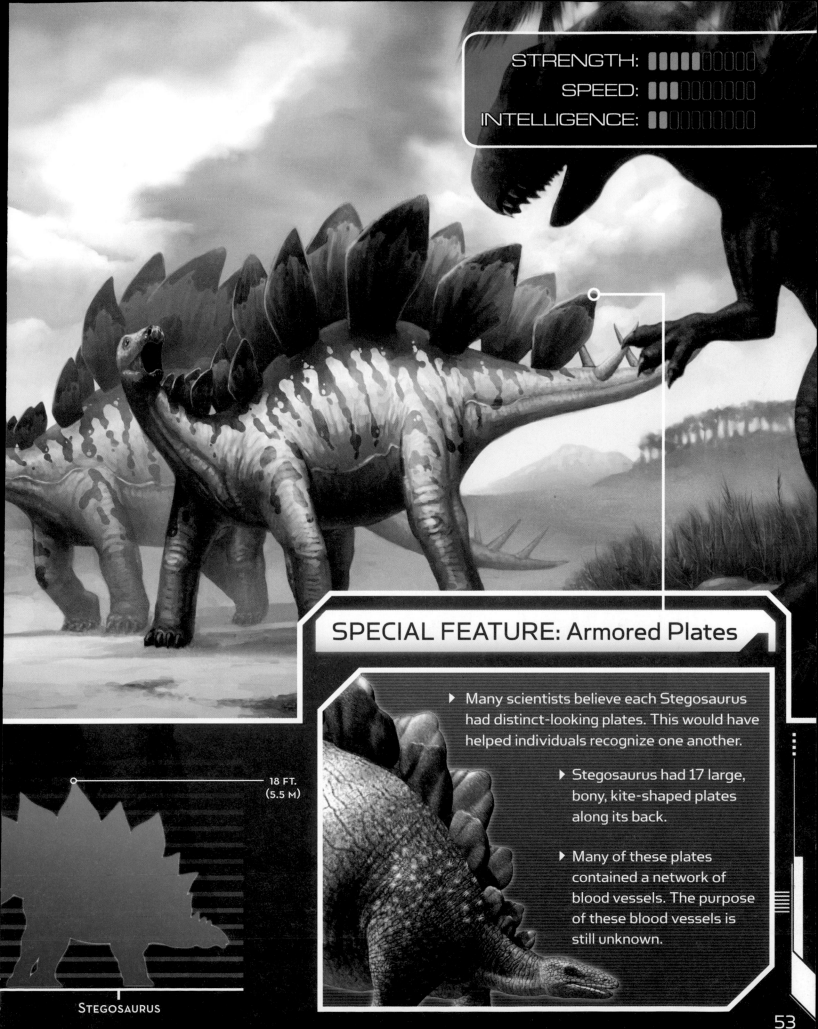

STRENGTH: ⬛⬛⬛⬛⬛☐☐☐☐☐
SPEED: ⬛⬛⬛☐☐☐☐☐☐☐
INTELLIGENCE: ⬛⬛☐☐☐☐☐☐☐☐

18 FT.
(5.5 M)

SPECIAL FEATURE: Armored Plates

▶ Many scientists believe each Stegosaurus had distinct-looking plates. This would have helped individuals recognize one another.

▶ Stegosaurus had 17 large, bony, kite-shaped plates along its back.

▶ Many of these plates contained a network of blood vessels. The purpose of these blood vessels is still unknown.

STEGOSAURUS

TENONTOSAURUS

(ten-ON-tuh-SOR-us) "Tendon lizard"

Tenontosaurus is known for the bony tendons that ran the length of its tail.

VITAL STATS

LENGTH: 23 FT. (7 M)
WEIGHT: 2,200 LBS. (1,000 KG)
PERIOD: EARLY CRETACEOUS
PLACE: MONTANA, UTAH, AND WYOMING

QUICK FACTS

▸ Tenontosaurus had a bony beak, which it used to bite off plants.

▸ Broken teeth of much smaller Deinonychus have been found in a Tenontosaurus skeleton. Scientists believe Deinonychus hunted the larger dinosaurs.

DINO-SIZE

Tenontosaurus was about twice as long as an American alligator.

AMERICAN ALLIGATOR

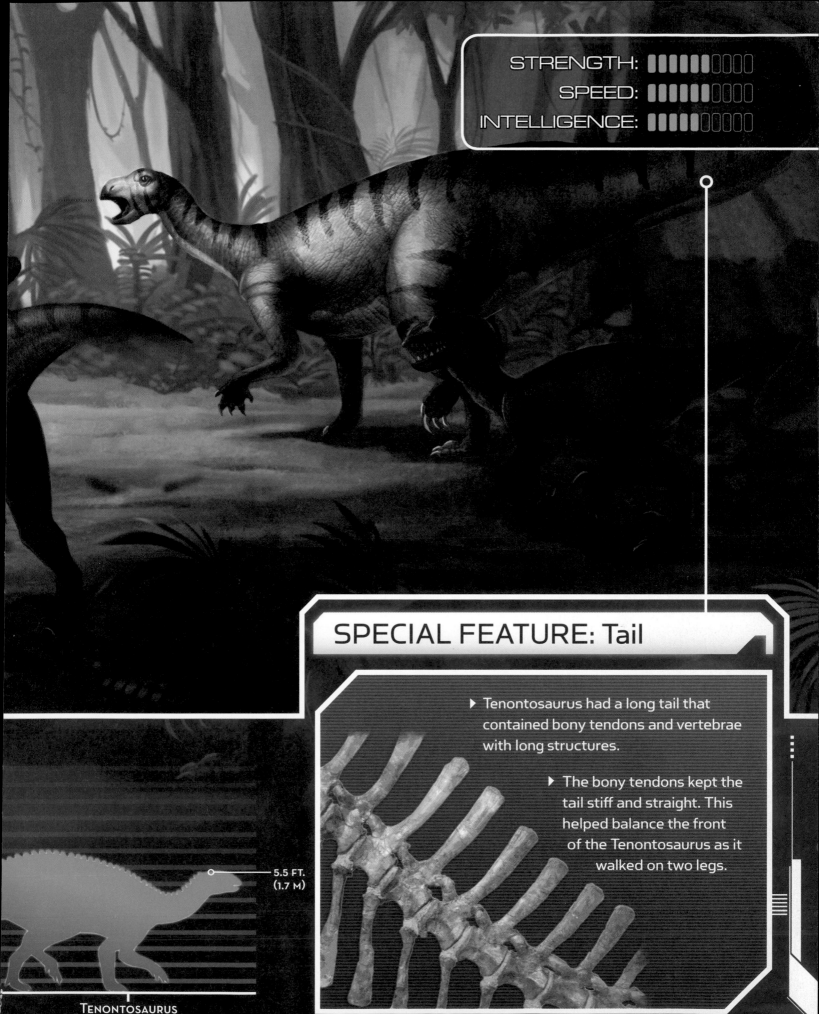

STRENGTH: ▮▮▮▮▮▮□□□□
SPEED: ▮▮▮▮▮▮□□□□
INTELLIGENCE: ▮▮▮▮▮□□□□□

SPECIAL FEATURE: Tail

▸ Tenontosaurus had a long tail that contained bony tendons and vertebrae with long structures.

▸ The bony tendons kept the tail stiff and straight. This helped balance the front of the Tenontosaurus as it walked on two legs.

5.5 FT. (1.7 M)

TENONTOSAURUS

THERIZINOSAURUS

(THAIR-uh-zee-nuh-SOR-us) "Scythe lizard"

The sharp-clawed Therizinosaurus is named after a scythe—a farm tool used for mowing grass and cutting crops.

QUICK FACTS

▶ Therizinosaurus most likely had a large neck, a small head, and a beaked mouth.

▶ Although the claws and hands of Therizinosaurus and related dinosaurs resembled those of meat-eating theropods, it's believed these dinosaurs might have been plant-eaters.

SPECIAL FEATURE: Claws

▶ Therizinosaurus had a claw on each of its three digits. The longest claw was over 23 in. (58 cm) long. That's about the length of a human arm.

▶ Because its claws are similar to the claws of some turtles, scientists originally thought Therizinosaurus bones they were studying belonged to a large turtle.

▶ Therizinosaurus may have used its claws to slash vegetation from trees.

DINO-SIZE

Therizinosaurus may have been four times the size of a horse.

27 FT. (8.2 M)

HORSE   THERIZINOSAURUS

VITAL STATS

LENGTH: ABOUT 33 FT. (10 M)
WEIGHT: ABOUT 2,200 LBS.
(1,000 KG)
PERIOD: LATE CRETACEOUS
PLACE: CENTRAL AND EAST ASIA

TRICERATOPS
(TRI-SARE-uh-tops) "THREE-HORNED FACE"

Triceratops was the dominant plant-eater of its time. With a broad, bony frill and three impressive horns, it could have fended off even the most ferocious predators.

VITAL STATS

LENGTH: UP TO 29 FT. (9 M)
WEIGHT: UP TO 22,000 LBS.
(10,000 KG)
PERIOD: LATE CRETACEOUS
PLACE: WESTERN U.S. AND
ALBERTA AND SASKATCHEWAN,
CANADA

QUICK FACTS

▸ Triceratops had teeth locked
together in rows, called batteries.
Beneath each tooth were other,
replacement teeth. Triceratops lost
and replaced teeth throughout its
lifetime, going through as many as
800 teeth.

▸ Scientists believe Triceratops
might have traveled in large herds.

Triceratops teeth

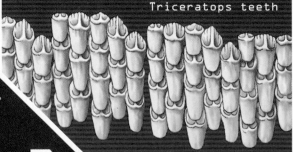

DINO-SIZE

Triceratops was about twice
as big as a white rhinoceros.

WHITE RHINOCEROS

STRENGTH: ▮▮▮▮▮▮▯▯▯▯

SPEED: ▮▮▮▯▯▯▯▯▯▯

INTELLIGENCE: ▮▮▮▮▮▯▯▯▯▯

9.5 FT.
(2.9 M)

TRICERATOPS

SPECIAL FEATURE: Frill

▸ The frill may have worked like an elephant's wide, flat ears to get rid of body heat.

▸ The frill provided places for huge jaw muscles to attach to the skull.

▸ Many scientists believe the frill was also used by males to attract females, in the same way that bucks use their antlers to attract does.

TYRANNOSAURUS REX

(TIE-RAN-uh-SOR-us REX) "TYRANT LIZARD KING"

With its powerful jaws and spiky, banana-sized teeth, Tyrannosaurus rex deserves its name.

VITAL STATS

LENGTH: ABOUT 40 FT. (12 M)
WEIGHT: 14,000 LBS.
(6,350 KG)
PERIOD: LATE CRETACEOUS
PLACE: WESTERN NORTH AMERICA

QUICK FACTS

▸ Although Tyrannosaurus rex was bipedal, it was unable to stand upright. Doing so would have placed enormous strain on its hips and spine.

▸ Tyrannosaurus rex could run up to 18 mph (29 kph). That's faster than a human but slower than a dog.

DINO-SIZE

Tyrannosaurus rex was about the length of a humpback whale.

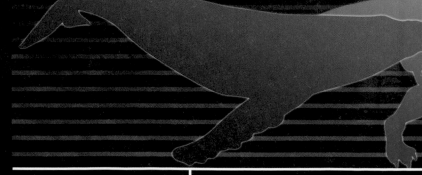

HUMPBACK WHALE

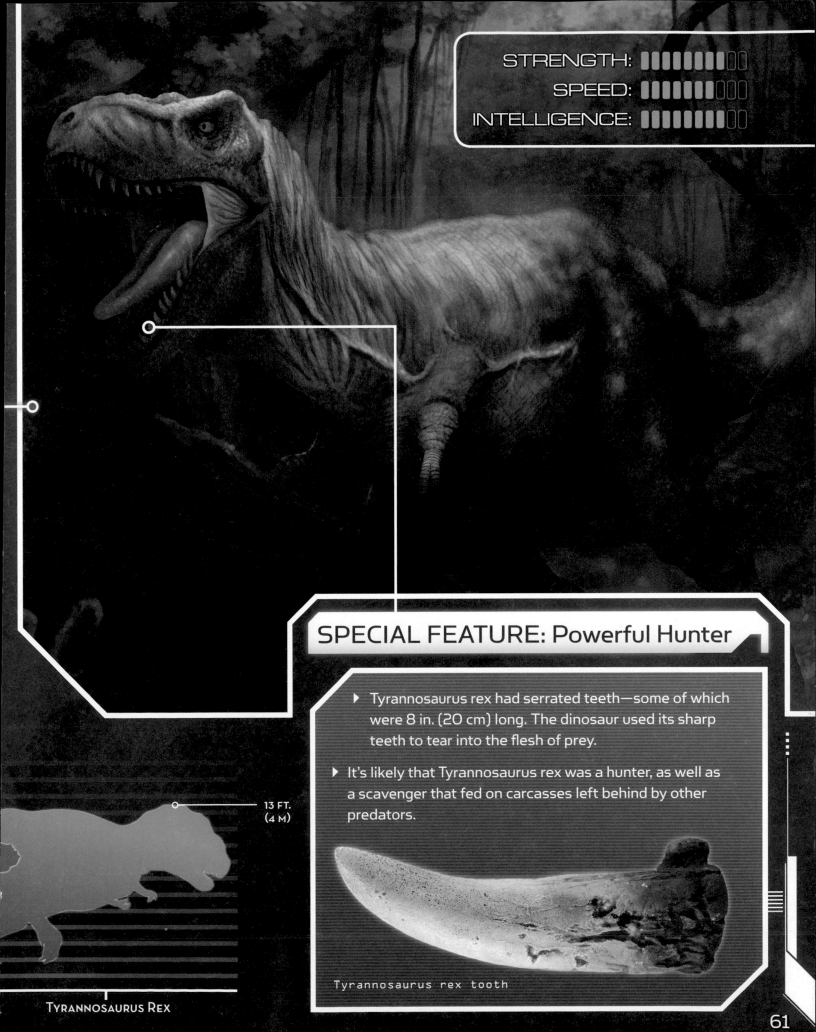

STRENGTH: ▮▮▮▮▮▮▮▮□□

SPEED: ▮▮▮▮▮▮□□□

INTELLIGENCE: ▮▮▮▮▮▮▮□□

13 FT.
(4 M)

SPECIAL FEATURE: Powerful Hunter

▸ Tyrannosaurus rex had serrated teeth—some of which were 8 in. (20 cm) long. The dinosaur used its sharp teeth to tear into the flesh of prey.

▸ It's likely that Tyrannosaurus rex was a hunter, as well as a scavenger that fed on carcasses left behind by other predators.

Tyrannosaurus rex tooth

TYRANNOSAURUS REX

TAWA HALLAE

(Ta-WA hall-A) named for Tawa, the Pueblo sun god, and fossil collector Ruth Hall

Tawa hallae was discovered in 2006, in the famous fossil site Ghost Ranch, New Mexico. News of this discovery was reported to the world in 2009.

Vital Stats

Length: 13 ft. (4 m)
Weight: Unknown
Period: Late Triassic
Place: New Mexico

Quick Facts

▸ Tawa belongs to an order of dinosaurs called theropods, which were bipedal and "lizard-hipped." Their hip structure was similar to that of modern lizards.

▸ Like other dinosaurs, Tawa had structures, called air sacs, in its neck and around its braincase. Though these structures are common in modern birds, the function of Tawa's is unknown.

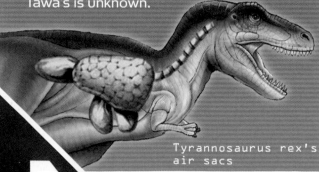

Tyrannosaurus rex's air sacs

Dino-Size

Tawa hallae was about twice the size of a grizzly bear.

Grizzly Bear

STRENGTH: ▮▮▮▮▮▯▯▯▯▯
SPEED: ▮▮▮▮▮▮▯▯▯▯
INTELLIGENCE: ▮▮▮▮▮▮▮▮▯▯

4 FT.
(1.2 M)

TAWA HALLAE

SPECIAL FEATURE:
Tawa's Ancestry

DINOSAURS

ORNITHISCHIANS

SAURISCHIANS

SAUROPODOMORPHS   THERAPODS

▸ Many of Tawa's features resemble those of early dinosaurs, which lived during the early Triassic period. The early dinosaurs lived in what is now South America.

▸ Eventually, these dinosaurs evolved into two lineages: saurischians—which include sauropodomorphs and carnivorous dinosaurs called theropods—and ornithischians. Tawa was a theropod.

▸ The different dinosaurs moved beyond "South America," and spread to other parts of the world.

GEOLOGICAL PERIODS

TRIASSIC PERIOD

During the Triassic period, much of Earth's land was locked together into a continent known as Pangaea (pan-GEE-uh). During this period, the supercontinent was starting to break apart. Triassic Earth was hot and dry. Even the North and South Poles were free of ice.

DINOSAURS FROM THE PERIOD:

- COELOPHYSIS
- TAWA HALLAE

JURASSIC PERIOD

200–146 MILLION YEARS AGO

During the Jurassic period, Pangaea broke up into two major continents, Laurasia to the north and Gondwana to the south. The world was still warm.

DINOSAURS FROM THE PERIOD:

- ARCHAEOPTERYX
- BAROSAURUS
- COMPSOGNATHUS
- DIPLODOCUS
- HETERODONTOSAURUS
- LIOPLEURODON
- SCUTELLOSAURUS
- SEISMOSAURUS
- STEGOSAURUS

CRETACEOUS PERIOD

146–65 MILLION YEARS AGO

During the Cretaceous period, the continents broke apart, forming the same continents we know today. In the early part of the Cretaceous, temperatures were lower, but they rose again for the rest of the period.

DINOSAURS FROM THE PERIOD:

- BARYONYX
- CARCHARODONTOSAURUS
- CARNOTAURUS
- DEINONYCHUS
- DROMICEIOMIMUS
- EUOPLOCEPHALUS
- GALLIMIMUS
- HYPSILOPHODON
- MAIASAURA
- MUTTABURRASAURUS
- OVIRAPTOR
- PACHYCEPHALOSAURUS
- PARASAUROLOPHUS
- PTERANODON
- SPINOSAURUS
- TENONTOSAURUS
- THERIZINOSAURUS
- TRICERATOPS
- TYRANNOSAURUS REX